Mar. 31, 2009

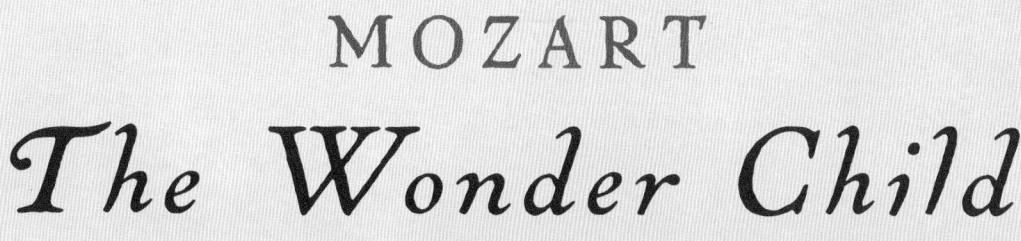

MOZART
The Wonder Child

A Puppet Play in Three Acts

JE
780.92
MOZ

M O Z

The Won

A Puppet Play in Three Acts

A R T

der Child

By Diane Stanley

Collins
An Imprint of HarperCollinsPublishers

*J*ohannes *Chrysostomus Wolfgang Gottlieb Mozart* was only three years old—not much bigger than his name— on the day his life changed forever.

Wonder Child

He was used to hearing music in the house. His papa, Leopold, was a musician. But that day Wolfgang heard something new. His big sister, Nannerl,♪ was learning to play the clavier.♪♪ Wolfgang wanted lessons too!

So he toddled over and joined them at the keyboard. He tried a few notes, then started picking out chords. Some of them sounded ugly to him, but others were incredibly beautiful. His face lit up with joy.

Seeing how excited little Wolfgang was, Papa tried teaching him a few simple pieces. Within the year he was reading music and could learn a minuet in half an hour.

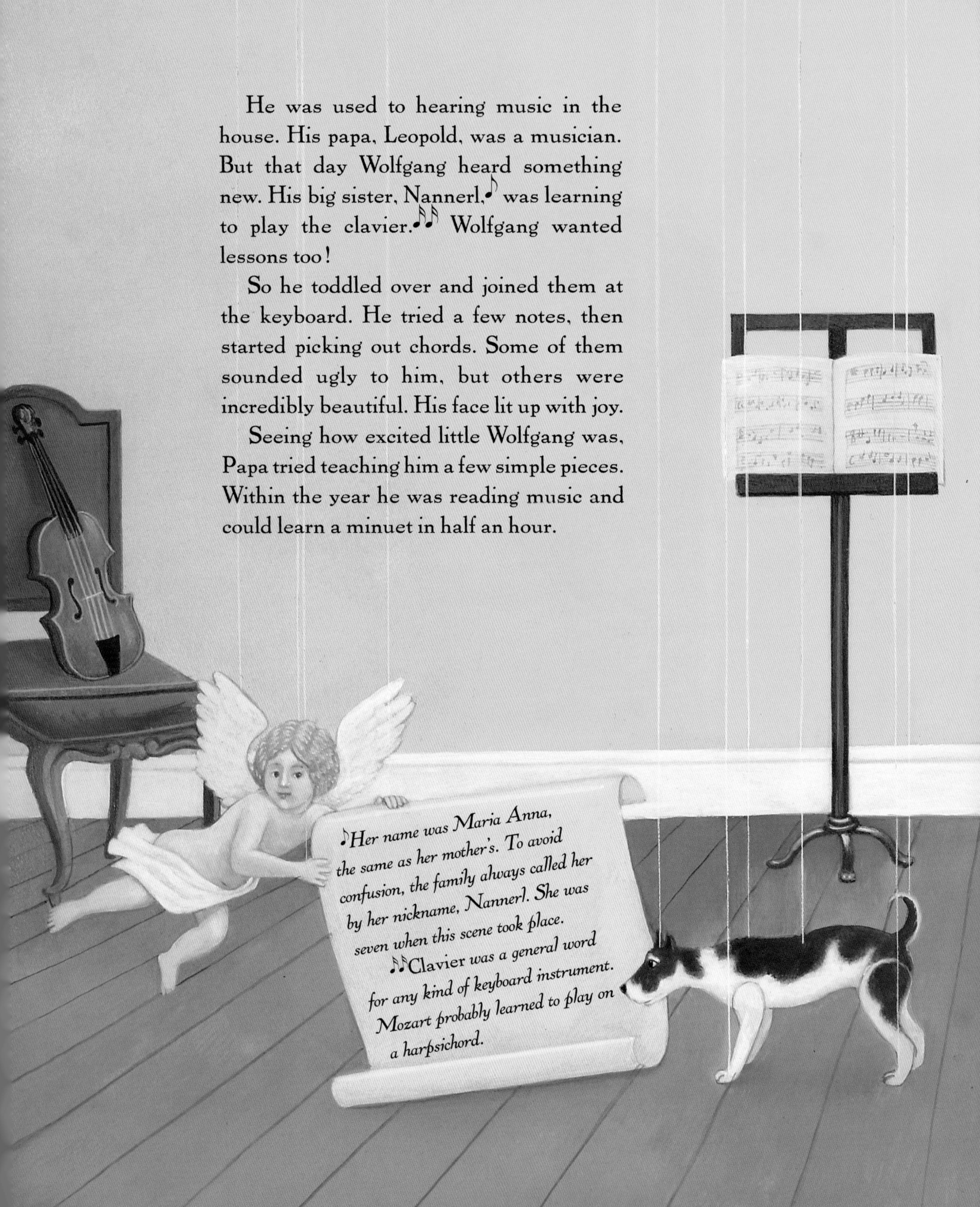

♪Her name was Maria Anna, the same as her mother's. To avoid confusion, the family always called her by her nickname, Nannerl. She was seven when this scene took place.
♪♪Clavier was a general word for any kind of keyboard instrument. Mozart probably learned to play on a harpsichord.

One morning, when Wolfgang was four, he decided to write some music. He hadn't learned how to use a quill pen yet, so he dipped it into the inkwell all the way. When he pulled the pen out, fat blobs of ink fell onto the music paper. He wiped them away with his hand and kept on working. Then Papa came home from church with a friend. "What are you writing?" Leopold asked.

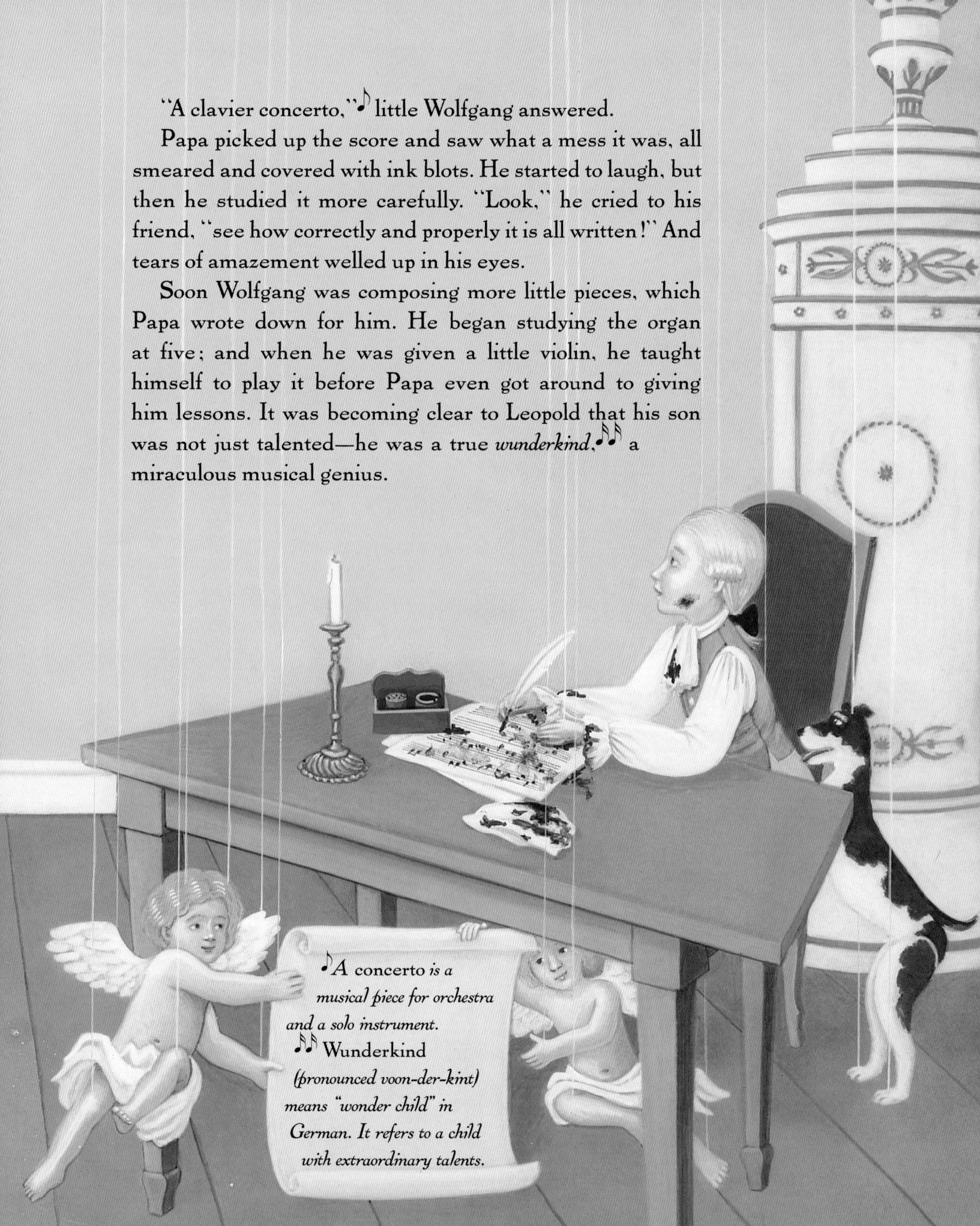

"A clavier concerto,"♪ little Wolfgang answered.

Papa picked up the score and saw what a mess it was, all smeared and covered with ink blots. He started to laugh, but then he studied it more carefully. "Look," he cried to his friend, "see how correctly and properly it is all written!" And tears of amazement welled up in his eyes.

Soon Wolfgang was composing more little pieces, which Papa wrote down for him. He began studying the organ at five; and when he was given a little violin, he taught himself to play it before Papa even got around to giving him lessons. It was becoming clear to Leopold that his son was not just talented—he was a true *wunderkind*,♪♪ a miraculous musical genius.

♪A concerto is a musical piece for orchestra and a solo instrument. ♪♪ Wunderkind (pronounced voon-der-kint) means "wonder child" in German. It refers to a child with extraordinary talents.

♪ The Archbishopric of Salzburg, where Mozart was born, was a German-speaking religious state west of Austria. It was ruled by Catholic archbishops who also held the title of prince. Its capital city, where the Mozarts lived, was also called Salzburg.

Meanwhile, Nannerl was showing great promise, too. She wasn't as precocious as her brother, but she still played amazingly well for a little girl. Leopold could hardly believe his good fortune: two prodigies in one family!

He decided not to send them to school, but to teach them himself. And he wouldn't keep them hidden away in Salzburg, ♪ either. He felt it was his duty to show them to the world, so that people would believe in miracles.

Leopold began by taking the children to Munich and Vienna, two of the great music capitals of Europe. In Vienna they gave a concert for Her Royal Highness Maria Theresa, empress of the Holy Roman Empire. The empress was delighted by six-year-old Wolfgang. He looked so sweet in his fancy suit and little powdered wig! She didn't even mind too much when he climbed up onto her lap and gave her a kiss!

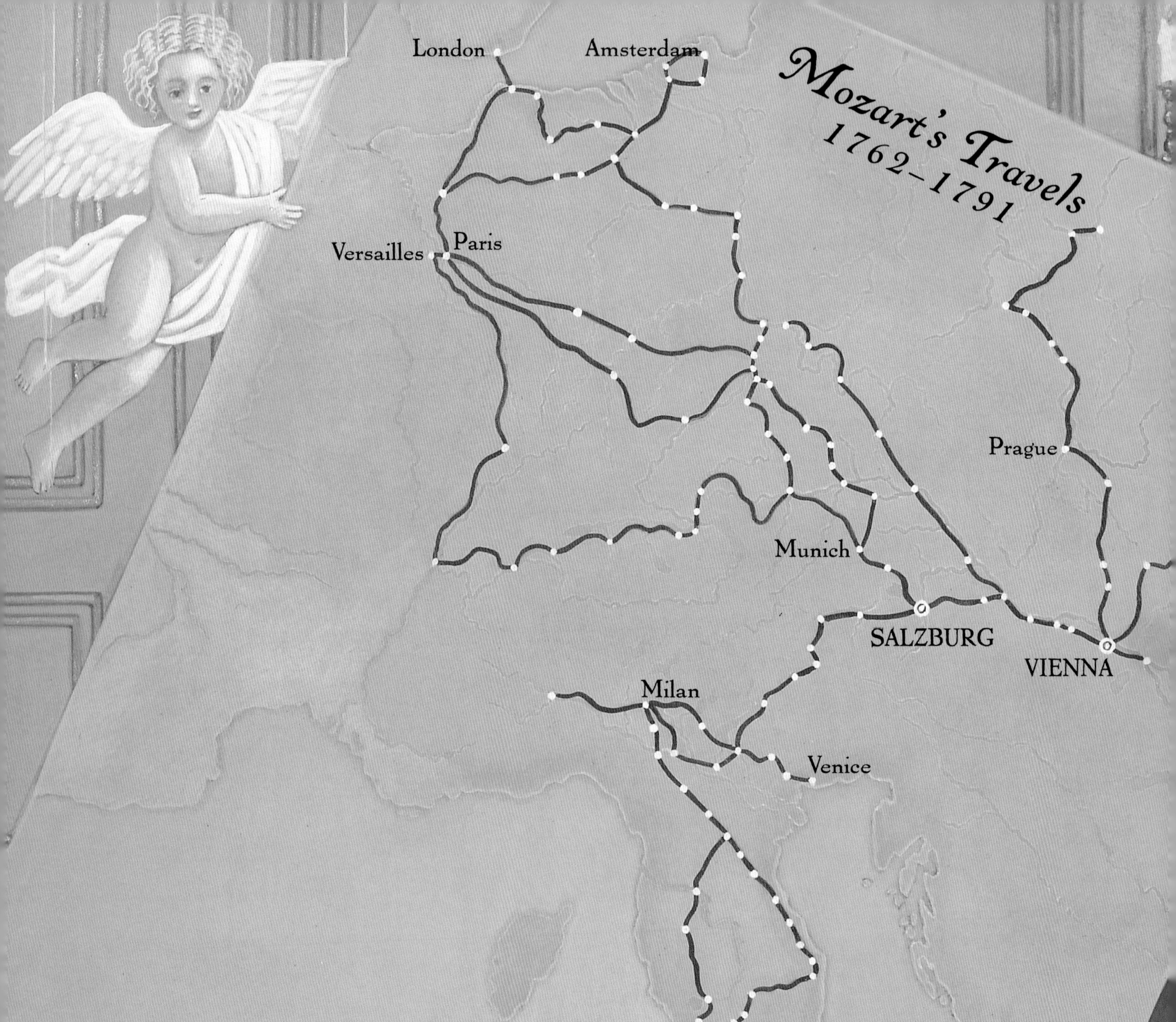

Mozart's Travels
1762–1791
London
Amsterdam
Versailles
Paris
Prague
Munich
SALZBURG
VIENNA
Milan
Venice
Rome
Naples

The concert for the empress went so well that Leopold decided to take the Mozart show on the road. He packed up his family and—together with a servant to help them get dressed in their complicated clothes and arrange and powder their complicated hairdos—set off on a tour of Europe. They made eighty-eight stops along the way (counting return visits) and were gone three and a half years.

Wolfgang gave performances, saw the
sights, and learned new languages. He
attended concerts and operas in many different
cities and was soon up-to-date in the latest styles of music.
He met famous musicians, such as Johann Christian Bach, who shared their
musical knowledge with him. It was the perfect education for a budding
musical genius.

The greatest families of Europe invited the Mozarts into their mansions and
palaces. The children played for King Louis XV of France and King George III
of England. They were rewarded for their concerts with money and expensive
gifts—golden swords, pocket watches, jewelry, fancy clothes, and other
precious trinkets.

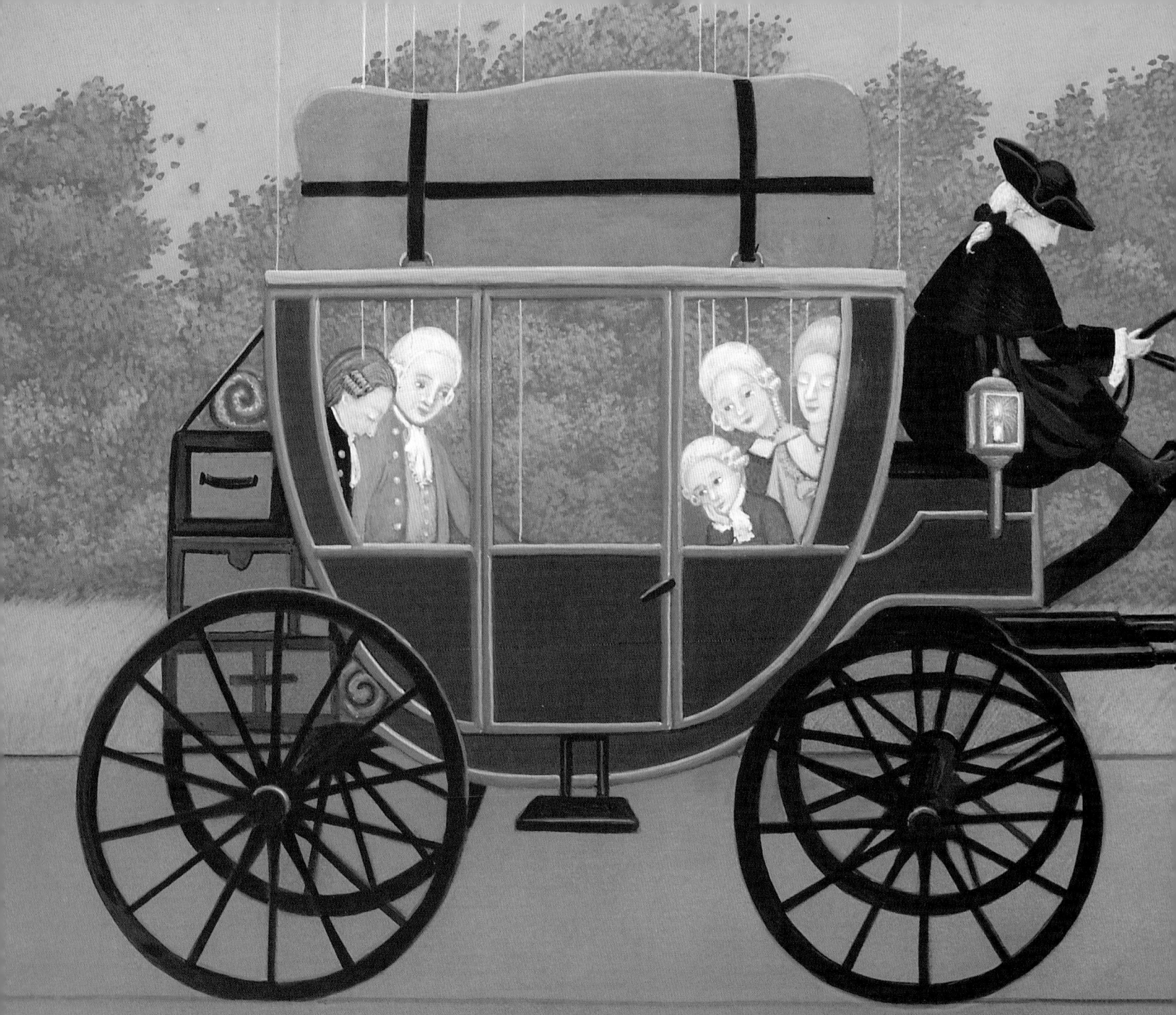

But life on tour wasn't always glamorous. They traveled thousands of miles in carriages with hard seats, over roads full of ruts and potholes. As the family rattled along, they were thrown against the walls of the coach (and each other) till they were bruised and aching. And the long drives could be horribly boring. To pass the time, the children invented a magical kingdom of which Wolfgang was the king and Nannerl was the queen. But at the end of the day, the little royals still had to sleep four to a room in a country inn, where there was likely to be no heat (but plenty of fleas and bedbugs).

Not surprisingly, everyone in the family got sick at one time or another, often with life-threatening diseases. Wolfgang himself suffered from smallpox and scarlet fever and nearly died of typhus.

In England, Leopold was very ill and everyone had to be quiet so he could rest. Since Wolfgang couldn't play the keyboard, he wrote his first symphony instead. Nannerl sat beside her eight-year-old brother, copying down the notes as he composed in his head. "Remind me to give something good to the horn," he said.

Of course, Wolfgang was the real star of the Mozart show. Everybody was talking about the amazing little boy who could play as well as a court musician. And he did tricks, too! He could play with the keyboard covered. He could reproduce a piece of music perfectly after hearing it only once. And his ear for music was so finely tuned that if you rang a bell or struck a glass with a spoon, he could tell you the exact note.

From Allegro in B flat for Keyboard

What a strange and magical childhood it must have been for Wolfgang, always in the spotlight, dressed like a doll in fancy clothes, being praised, petted, and covered with kisses by the greatest nobles of Europe. By the age of six, he was already the primary breadwinner for his family. In a single concert he made twice as much as Papa earned in a year back home. How powerful he must have felt!

Pupille amate from Lucio Silla

The family went home at the end of the tour, but they didn't stay there long. Soon they were off again. After a disastrous trip to Vienna (where they hardly made any money and the children both caught smallpox), Leopold set his sights on Italy, the birthplace of opera. He thought Wolfgang, now thirteen, ought to be exposed to Italian music. He might even be invited to write an opera. But this time, in the interest of saving money, Leopold decided to leave the women behind. It must have been a terrible blow to Nannerl, who had always been part of the Mozart show. But she never questioned her father's decisions. "After God comes Papa" had always been the family motto.

For four wonderful years, father and son shuttled back and forth between dreary Salzburg and sunny Italy, where Wolfgang played at the homes of dukes and princes, attended concerts, and dressed up in costume for carnival balls. He was made a Knight of the Golden Order by Pope Clement XIV and was invited to write not one but three operas for the theater of Milan. It was a truly magical time in Wolfgang's life. In that beautiful, musical place, he left childhood behind and came into his own as a mature musician.

♪Carnival was a period of merrymaking between Christmas and Lent, celebrated in Catholic countries. It was the season for musical events, such as operas, and people often went to parties wearing costumes and masks.

Allegro moderato

from Symphony No. 29 in A Major

And then the glory days were over. The theater in Milan didn't ask Wolfgang to write another opera. They moved on to somebody new. Nor did any of the noblemen they met on their travels offer him a job. No one knows exactly why.

Wolfgang's age was certainly part of it—at seventeen, he was too old to be a prodigy, yet still considered too young for an important position. But the family's reputation may have been part of it, too. Leopold offended people with the boorish and pushy way he promoted his children. And Wolfgang's confidence and high spirits made him seem arrogant and disrespectful. (If only he had "half the talent and twice the manners," one exasperated friend complained.) Their former patron, Maria Theresa, had grown totally disenchanted, calling the Mozarts "useless people . . . who go about the world like beggars."

So now, having no better options, Leopold and Wolfgang went home to Salzburg to work for the prince-archbishop, a haughty man who considered his musicians to be servants and treated them with contempt. Wolfgang, who had kissed an empress, been knighted by the Pope, and been praised by kings and princes, found this very hard to bear.

♪ The previous archbishop had been generous about giving Leopold time off to take his children on tour. But he had recently died, and the new archbishop, Hieronymus Colloredo, was not nearly so understanding.

Leopold didn't like Salzburg any more than Wolfgang did. It was a small, provincial town with no opera and no theater. In great cities like Munich or Vienna, there were lots of aristocrats with the money and the taste to hire musicians. But in Salzburg it was the hated archbishop and his court, or nothing at all. Leopold still hoped his brilliant son would get a good job in some big city. Then the whole family could leave Salzburg and join him there, and he could support them. But the years passed and nothing of the sort materialized. They decided it was time to show the

world what an incredible musician the former wonder child had become. Then maybe something would finally happen. So Wolfgang quit his job in Salzburg and, for the last time, headed off on tour.

But Leopold didn't trust his son to travel alone. The boy wasn't practical. He was too trusting and couldn't handle money. Since the archbishop wouldn't give Leopold time off from work, Wolfgang—a grown man of twenty-one—had to go on tour under the tender care of his mother.

Wolfgang left in high spirits, thrilled to be out of Salzburg and traveling again. But the purpose of his trip was to find a job, and in this he was soon disappointed. As before, nobody offered him anything, though at one low point he swallowed his pride and begged a German prince for a job. "Allow me to dare lay myself most humbly at your feet and offer you my services," he said.

"My dear child," came the reply, "there is no vacancy here."

And so the situation was already grim by the time they reached Paris—at which point things got drastically worse. Maria Anna wasn't feeling well, but she refused to see a French doctor. By the time Wolfgang found a German one, she had taken a turn for the worse. It probably didn't matter; the medicine he gave her (rhubarb powder mixed with wine) was as useless as most medical treatment of the time. On the night of July 3, 1778, Maria Anna Mozart died. It was probably the darkest moment of Wolfgang's life.

Sixteen months after leaving Salzburg so full of hope, his mother by his side, Wolfgang returned home alone, brokenhearted and dejected, to face his angry father and enter a life of "slavery" to the prince-archbishop.

Then, after a year and a half in the suffocating atmosphere of Salzburg, Wolfgang got a reprieve. He was invited to write an opera for the famous Munich Theater, a tremendous honor!

Idomeneo was to be an Italian opera based on a French play, so they needed someone fluent in both languages to write the *libretto.* Wolfgang found such a person in Salzburg—then proceeded to give him endless suggestions for making the characters richer and the story more effective on the stage.

With the libretto more or less finished, Wolfgang left for Munich to work on the music. The first thing he did was meet his singers, to find out what kind of voices they had and whether or not they could act. Mozart said he liked to fit his arias to the singers "like a well-made suit of clothes." But he didn't just write the music. He oversaw the rehearsals with infinite care. He wanted his operas to be more than just pretty costumes and beautiful music. He wanted stories that felt real, that came alive on the stage and touched the heart of the audience.

from Se il padre perdei - Idomeneo

♪ The people of Munich spoke German, but operas were traditionally sung in Italian, considered the "language of opera."

♪♪ Libretto means "little book" in Italian. Like the script of a play, the libretto is the story of an opera, with dialogue and words for the arias, or songs.

Wolfgang had been given six weeks off from his job to go to Munich and write his opera. But six weeks had stretched into four months, and the archbishop was running out of patience. He was on a long visit to Vienna, and he wanted his best keyboard player there so he could show him off to his noble guests. Mozart must come immediately!

He went, but after his triumph in Munich, Wolfgang was in no mood to bow and scrape and be humble. When he was ordered to wait outside the archbishop's apartments every morning (in case the great man should want a bit of music), Mozart snapped. He simply refused to do it. Naturally the archbishop was outraged. Wolfgang was his servant and should do as he was told.

"If you will not serve me properly, then clear out," he roared. "I will have nothing more to do with such a rogue."

"Nor I any longer with you!" Mozart spat back.

And so, in the end, Wolfgang got his wish. He wasn't merely asked to leave the archbishop's service; he was literally kicked out the door.

With that kick, Wolfgang Mozart became a free man.

Mozart stayed on in Vienna, where he would live for the rest of his life. He knew it wasn't going to be easy to make a living on his own, without a regular salary from a patron. But he was willing to work hard. He got up every morning at six, when his hairdresser came to curl, style, and powder his hair. By seven he was dressed and ready to plunge into a full schedule of teaching, composing, and performing. Since he had a lot of friends and liked to visit them frequently, his days were full indeed. Most nights he didn't get to bed till one, then was up at six the next morning, ready to start again.

He did everything he could think of to make money. He gave music lessons, entertained at private parties, and wrote and played piano concertos for the public. (Since people weren't interested in "old" music in those days, he had to write a new concerto for each performance.) He composed symphonies for large orchestras, arias for concert singers, and trios, quartets, and quintets for amateur musicians to play at home with their families and friends. He even wrote dance tunes for the ballrooms of Vienna. And it all paid off. That first year he earned twice as much as the archbishop had been paying him—and he would never make less for the rest of his life.

Now that he had his freedom and a fairly steady income, all he lacked was a wife.

♪ A patron is a wealthy person who supports writers, artists, or musicians.
♪♪ The name piano is short for pianoforte, which means "soft-loud" in Italian. It was a new instrument at the time, and unlike the harpsichord, it could play both soft and loud notes. Mozart helped to make the piano popular through his concerts.

Years before, while on tour with his mother, Wolfgang had fallen in love with a beautiful singer, Aloysia Weber. She rejected him, but he remained close to her family. For a while, after the archbishop kicked him out of the palace, Wolfgang rented a room in the Webers' house. Aloysia was married and gone by then, but her three sisters were still at home. And that is how, once again, Wolfgang gave his heart to a Weber girl. Only this time he got it right.

Constanze was not as pretty as Aloysia, or as fine a singer. But she and Wolfgang had the same lively, fun-loving nature. And she was a practical girl, sensible and thrifty. He thought she would make an excellent wife. And so, at the age of twenty-six, Wolfgang married Constanze. "When we were joined together," he wrote, "my wife and I began to cry—everyone was touched by it, even the priest."

They would share good times and hard times in their life together. Of the six children they brought into the world, only two—Carl Thomas and Franz Xaver—would survive. They would live too lavishly and fall into debt. And now and then they would be angry with each other. But on the whole, they had a profoundly happy marriage.

The Mozarts had a dog named Wimperl and a starling called Stahrl, who could whistle the theme from Wolfgang's piano concerto in G Major.

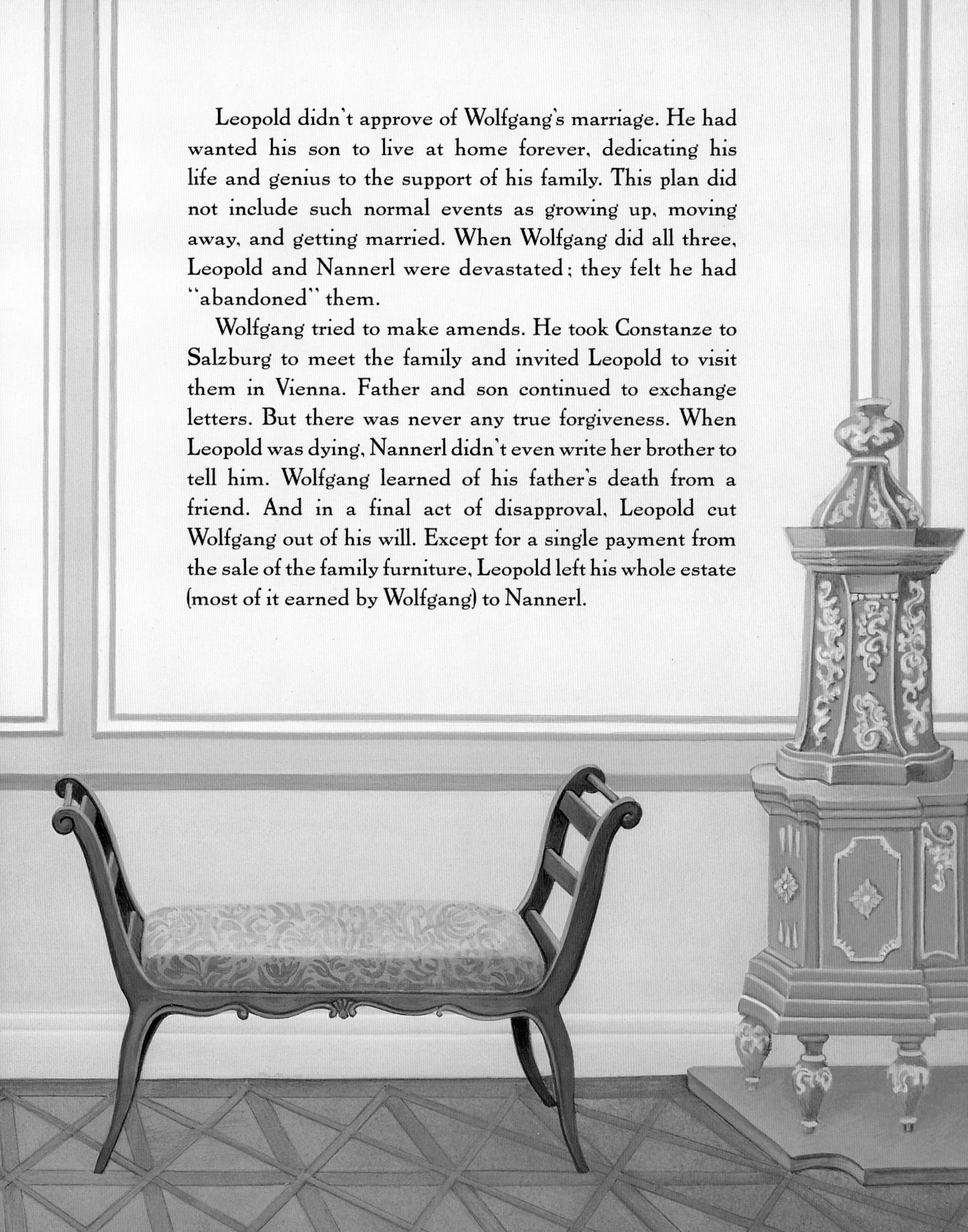

Leopold didn't approve of Wolfgang's marriage. He had wanted his son to live at home forever, dedicating his life and genius to the support of his family. This plan did not include such normal events as growing up, moving away, and getting married. When Wolfgang did all three, Leopold and Nannerl were devastated; they felt he had "abandoned" them.

Wolfgang tried to make amends. He took Constanze to Salzburg to meet the family and invited Leopold to visit them in Vienna. Father and son continued to exchange letters. But there was never any true forgiveness. When Leopold was dying, Nannerl didn't even write her brother to tell him. Wolfgang learned of his father's death from a friend. And in a final act of disapproval, Leopold cut Wolfgang out of his will. Except for a single payment from the sale of the family furniture, Leopold left his whole estate (most of it earned by Wolfgang) to Nannerl.

Wolfgang first made his name in Vienna as a pianist. But with time, he grew tired of being an entertainer. More and more, he longed to be known as a composer. And of all the things there were to compose, Mozart loved opera best. Unfortunately, it was an expensive business, not something you could put together on your own. You had to be invited to

Allegro from *Come scoglio – Così fan tutte*

♪Da Ponte left Vienna after his third collaboration with Mozart. He ended up in America, where he became the first professor of Italian literature at Columbia College in New York.

Così fan tutte

write an opera, by some great patron or a theater company with plenty of money to invest.

Now, as Mozart was reaching his full maturity, everything fell into place. The invitations came. And at the same time, he found his perfect collaborator, the Italian librettist Lorenzo Da Ponte.♪ Together, they created three of the most beloved and frequently performed operas of all time: *The Marriage of Figaro*, *Don Giovanni*, and *Così fan tutte*. If Mozart had written nothing else in his life, they would still have made him immortal.

Mozart had always worked hard. Now he was moving at a frantic pace, with two operas opening in two cities within a single month—*La Clemenza di Tito* in Prague and *The Magic Flute* in Vienna. It must have been exhausting.

Yet composing *The Magic Flute* was a true labor of love for Mozart. He enjoyed the opera so much that after conducting the first two performances himself, he continued to go almost every night, reveling in his own glorious music, delighting in the laughter and applause of the audience.

♪The Magic Flute was actually a singspiel, or "sung play," with spoken dialogue and the words in German, the language of the people who were hearing it, much like a modern Broadway musical.

One night Mozart decided to play a trick on one of his friends, the owner of the theater and author of the libretto. This man was also a singer and was playing the important role of Papageno, the bird-man. In several scenes, Papageno played his magical bells—though the actual sound came from a glockenspiel offstage. Mozart started playing the glockenspiel when Papageno wasn't even touching the bells. The friend, catching on, glared fiercely at the bells and ordered them to "Shut up!" Mozart loved it, and so did the crowd.

While Mozart was enjoying his playful new opera, he was hard at work on a far more somber kind of music. A servant had appeared at the house several months before with a commission from his master, who wished to remain anonymous. He offered to pay Mozart handsomely to write a requiem, a musical setting of the Catholic mass for the dead. The business was secretive and the terms unusual. Though Mozart didn't know it, there was a definite reason for all this mystery: his patron, an eccentric count, liked to hire composers to write music that he would then recopy in his own hand and pretend to have written himself. The count's wife had recently died, and he planned to "compose" Mozart's requiem in her honor.

Mozart accepted this strange commission but put off working on it; he had two operas to finish first. By the time he was able to turn his full attention to the requiem, he was exhausted from overwork and in a growing state of gloom and depression. He became obsessed with the grim idea that he was writing his own funeral mass. Then his health began to fail and he took to his bed. Still, he continued to work feverishly on the *Requiem*; he needed to finish it so he could get paid. When he could no longer hold a pen, his pupil Franz Xaver Süssmayr sat by his side and wrote the notes down for him—just as Leopold and Nannerl had done when Wolfgang was a little child.

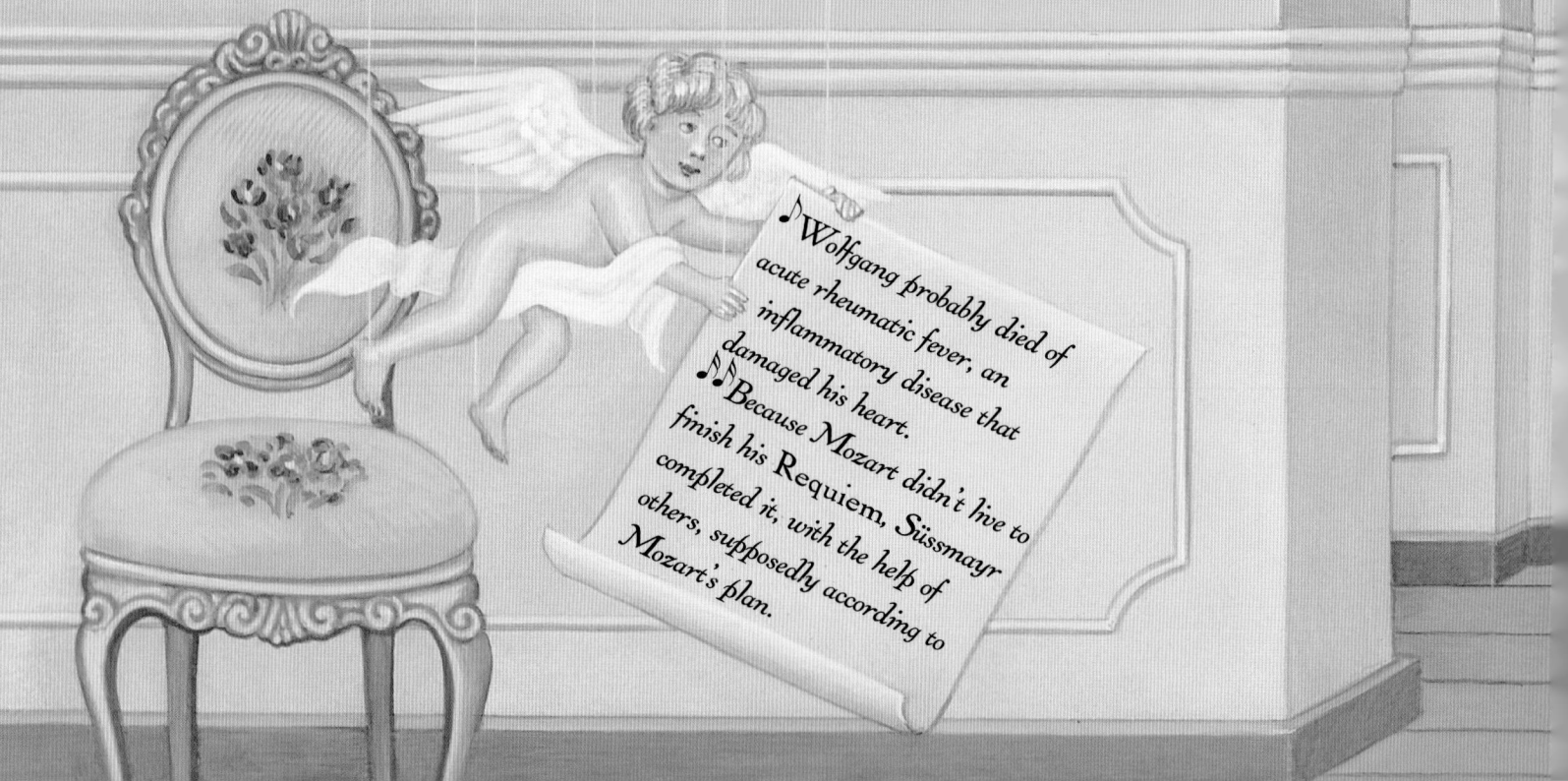

Wolfgang probably died of acute rheumatic fever, an inflammatory disease that damaged his heart. Because Mozart didn't live to finish his Requiem, Süssmayr completed it, with the help of others, supposedly according to Mozart's plan.

One afternoon, Wolfgang had himself propped up in bed and, together with three friends, sang through the still unfinished *Requiem*. Perhaps he wept as he sang—Mozart was a tenderhearted man, quick to tears, and he knew that he was dying. The music surely filled his soul as no music had before, so movingly does it express the finality of death, the fear of judgment, and the awesome majesty of God.

That night he fell into a troubled sleep and dreamed of music. He thought he was back at the theater, hearing *The Magic Flute*. One of Constanze's sisters, the soprano Josepha Hofer, was singing her dazzling aria as Queen of the Night. "Quiet, quiet!" Mozart whispered. "Hofer is taking her top F!"

Then the bell-like tones of Josepha's voice were replaced in his mind by the thunderous "Dies irae" from the *Requiem*: "*Day of wrath! Day of doom!*" He puffed out his cheeks, imitating the sound of the drums.

And then, shortly after midnight on December 5, 1791, at the tragically young age of thirty-five, Wolfgang Mozart rose on the wings of music to his eternal resting place. He left behind a glorious legacy, a priceless gift of more than six hundred musical works, so full of power, invention, and sheer, breathtaking beauty that it has astounded the world ever since.

Now it is yours to discover.

MOZART'S NAMES

Mozart never used his first two names, Johannes Chrysostomus, which honored the saint on whose feast day he was born. But he was very fond of his middle name, Gottlieb, which means "loved by God" in German. He was christened with the Latinized Greek version, Wolfgangus *Theophilus*, but later changed it to the Italian Wolfgang *Amadeo*. Finally he settled on the French Wolfgang *Amadé*, which became his favorite. He did not use the Latin *Amadeus*, by which people know him today.

THE SALZBURG MARIONETTES

While in Austria doing research for this book, I visited the famous Salzburg Marionette Theatre and was inspired to present Mozart's life as a puppet play in three acts. The Salzburg Marionette Theatre was established more than ninety years ago, and its first production was Mozart's early opera *Bastien and Bastienne*. Since then, the exquisitely carved and lavishly dressed Salzburg marionettes have performed all over the world, specializing in simplified versions of operas, but especially those of the city's favorite son, Wolfgang Mozart.

IMPORTANT DATES IN MOZART'S LIFE

1751	Maria Anna Mozart (Nannerl) is born in Salzburg on July 30–31.
1756	Wolfgang Gottlieb Mozart is born in Salzburg on January 27.
1760	(Age 4) Wolfgang's first attempt at composing.
1762	(Age 6) Wolfgang and Nannerl perform for the Empress Maria Theresa in Vienna.
1763	(Age 7) The Mozart family departs on their grand tour.
1764	(Age 8) Wolfgang publishes his first music in Paris.
1766	(Age 10) Family returns home to Salzburg at the end of November.
1768	(Age 12) *Bastien and Bastienne* opens in Vienna.
1769	(Age 13) *La finta semplice* (*The Pretend Simpleton*) opens in Salzburg.
1770	(Age 14) Wolfgang is made a Knight of the Golden Order by Pope Clement XIV; *Mitridate, re di Ponto* (*Mithridates, King of Pontus*) opens in Milan.
1771	(Age 15) *Ascanio in Alba* opens in Milan.
1772	(Age 16) Hieronymus Colloredo becomes the new prince-archbishop of Salzburg; Wolfgang is appointed concertmaster; his third and final Milanese opera, *Lucio Silla*, opens.
1773–1777	(Ages 17–21) Mostly in Salzburg; *La finta giardiniera* (*The Pretend Garden Girl*) opens in Munich, 1775.
1777	(Age 21) Wolfgang and his mother leave on the second grand tour; meets the Weber family and falls in love with Aloysia.
1778	(Age 22) Composes the *Paris* Symphony; Maria Anna Mozart dies on July 3 in Paris at the age of 57; Wolfgang is rejected by Aloysia.
1779	(Age 23) Returns to Salzburg in January; appointed court organist.

1781	(Age 25) *Idomeneo* opens in Munich; Wolfgang is dismissed by Archbishop Colloredo and settles in Vienna; begins courting Constanze.
1782	(Age 26) *Die Entführung aus dem Serail* (*The Abduction from the Harem*) opens in Vienna; marries Constanze Weber on August 4.
1783	(Age 27) Their first child, Raimund Leopold Mozart, is born and dies two months later, while Wolfgang and Constanze are away in Salzburg visiting the Mozart family; writes the *Linz* Symphony.
1784	(Age 28) Their second child, Carl Thomas, is born September 21.
1785	(Age 29) Leopold Mozart visits his son in Vienna from February to April.
1786	(Age 30) *Le nozze di Figaro* (*The Marriage of Figaro*) opens in Vienna; their third child, Johann Thomas Leopold Mozart, is born in October and dies in November.
1787	(Age 31) Composes the *Prague* Symphony; Wolfgang's father, Leopold Mozart, dies in Salzburg on May 28 at the age of 67; composes *Eine kleine Nachtmusik* (*A Little Night Music*); *Don Giovanni* opens in Prague; Emperor Joseph appoints Wolfgang Imperial Chamber Musician; their fourth child, Theresia Mozart, is born in December and dies six months later.
1789	(Age 33) Their fifth child, Anna Maria Mozart, is born and dies on November 16.
1790	(Age 34) *Così fan tutte* (*All Women Are like That*) opens in Vienna.
1791	(Age 35) Their sixth and last child, Franz Xaver Wolfgang Mozart, is born on July 26; Wolfgang receives an anonymous commission to write a requiem; *La clemenza di Tito* (*The Clemency of Titus*) opens in Prague on September 6; *Die Zauberflöte* (*The Magic Flute*) opens in Vienna on September 30; at work on the *Requiem* when he becomes too ill to continue; dies on December 5, is buried on December 7. A memorial service for Mozart is held in Vienna, where the unfinished *Requiem* is performed.

BIBLIOGRAPHY

Cairns, David. *Mozart and His Operas*. Berkeley, Los Angeles: University of California Press, 2006.

Glover, Jane. *Mozart's Women: His Family, His Friends, His Music*. New York: HarperCollins, 2005.

Gutman, Robert W. *Mozart: A Cultural Biography*. San Diego, New York, and London: Harcourt, 1999.

Landon, H. C. Robbins. *1791: Mozart's Last Year*. New York: Thames and Hudson, 1999.

Rushton, Julian. *Mozart*. Oxford and New York: Oxford University Press, 2006.

Sadie, Stanley. *Mozart: The Early Years, 1756–1781*. New York: W. W. Norton, 2006.

Solomon, Maynard. *Mozart: A Life*. New York: HarperPerennial, 1995.

Spaethling, Robert, ed. and trans. *Mozart's Letters, Mozart's Life: Selected Letters*. New York and London: W. W. Norton, 2000.

Sincere thanks to John J. H. Muller of the Juilliard School for his helpful review of the text and illustrations, and to Thomas O'Connor, General Director of the Santa Fe Pro Musica, for his kind assistance in choosing the music.

For Molly

MOZART: THE WONDER CHILD
A Puppet Play in Three Acts
Copyright © 2009 by Diane Stanley Manufactured in China.
For information address HarperCollins Children's
Books, a division of HarperCollins Publishers, 1350 Avenue of the Americas,
New York, NY 10019. www.harpercollinschildrens.com
Library of Congress Cataloging-in-Publication Data is available.
ISBN 978-0-06-072674-4 (trade bdg.) ISBN 978-0-06-072676-8
(lib. bdg.) Designed by Stephanie Bart-Horvath
1 2 3 4 5 6 7 8 9 10 ❖ First Edition